Bronze – Silver – Gold

Earning the Highest Awards

in Scouting

~

For Girls and Their Parents

~

Rae Brewer

Copyright © 2018 Rae Brewer

The opinions herein are solely those of the author and not endorsed by GSUSA.

Email Rae Brewer: kindredsoul65@gmail.com

Table of Contents

Preface: My Girl Scout Journey...5

The Highest Awards in Girl Scouting 9

The Bronze Award 14

The Silver Award 25

The Gold Award 34

National Young Women of Distinction.............................53

Monetary Rules...56

Choosing a Project...59

Project Ideas 63

Helicopter Parents 70

When Plans Go Awry...72

Gold Award Scholarships...75

Notes 77

Preface: My Girl Scout Journey

My own Girl Scout journey started when I was a child. Girl Scouts was very different back then. There wasn't a level called Daisies. I spent one year as a Brownie, three as a Junior and one as a Cadette. Unfortunately, by then, most girls had dropped out and there wasn't a troop for me to join. So I waved goodbye to scouting until, in 1992, I saw a blurb in the local newspaper stating that Girl Scouts was looking for volunteers.

I remembered with fondness the 5 years I spent in scouts as a young girl. So with visions of camping, cookies and crafts dancing in my head, I called the number listed. That phone call led to a 26-year whirlwind journey as an adult volunteer that started in Nation's Capital and still continues today in South Florida!

For much of those 26 years, I've been a Troop Leader. For the first six years, I led a troop eventhough I had NO children of my own!

When I finally birthed a child, I gave up the Troop Leader position for ten years. However, during that time, I continued working exclusively with adults rather than girls.

During those years I held many volunteer positions: Service Unit Manager, Service Unit Cookie Manager, Association Cookie Manager, Orientation Specialist, Organizer, Science Instructor, Registrar, Service Unit Treasurer, Council Program Volunteer, New Leader Coach, and Gold Award Advisor. At times, I filled four or five positions at once!

Finally, when my youngest was of age, I once again became a Troop Leader…and I've been leading Troop 10909 for over eleven years now.

This past scout year, in what must've been some type of psychotic break, I decided to start a new

Daisy troop! No, crazy as it seems, I do not have a Daisy-aged child. And, yes, that means that I am now the Leader of TWO troops in TWO different Service Units!

Suffice it to say, I've filled a LOT of positions in Girl Scouts, including leading troops at all levels.

My two daughters are also Girl Scouts. My oldest started in Daisies at the age of 4. (It was a one-year pilot program that allowed girls to start at 4 instead of 5.) She continued through to graduation and then became a Lifetime Member. In the 14 years she was a girl member, she earned the Bronze, Silver and Gold Awards.

My youngest daughter is currently an Ambassador scout. She's been in scouting since Kindergarten. She has also earned her Bronze and Silver Awards, but has not yet completed the Gold.

So now, I'd like to bring our expertise to you. My wish was to put together a volume that would guide girls and parents in their journey to earning the highest level awards.

All Councils have mandatory Gold Award classes to cover the basics. Most also offer optional classes for the Silver Award. This volume enriches that training, going into more detail and answering many questions that both girls and parents may have, even after attending a workshop. It gives loads of project ideas, for not only the Gold Award, but also the Silver and Bronze.

Here, in one guide, is a wealth of information to assist you in easily achieving a plan for an amazing Bronze, Silver and/or Gold Award Project.

If you take ONE thing away from reading this book, I hope it is this: You CAN do it!

I welcome and look forward to your questions, comments and suggestions! Email me at: kindredsoul65@gmail.com

The Highest Awards in Girl Scouting

The Bronze, Silver and Gold Awards are national Girl Scout Awards, given by local Councils, but with national standards set by GSUSA. However, despite the fact that they are national awards with national standards, every Council seems to be different in how they implement the procedures for earning the awards. Some Councils seem rather lax compared to others that seem to be sticklers.

Regardless of the Council, girls who earn these awards demonstrate many leadership skills that are valued throughout the world.

Published numbers on how many girls actually earn the Bronze or the Silver are difficult to find. But less than 6% of eligible girls earn the Gold! This is unfortunate. Not only will a stellar Gold Award Project stand out on college applications, and help girls earn scholarships, but the journey to Gold teaches knowledge and skills girls will use again and again in life: goal setting, decision making, critical thinking, leadership, time management, budgeting, advocacy, teamwork, problem solving, communication, personal development, management, public speaking, community involvement, and so much more!

Perhaps girls, and especially parents, aren't being educated on the benefits of earning the Gold. Perhaps girls and their parents are overwhelmed by the prospect of earning the Gold, thinking it too daunting of a task. Perhaps girls are just too busy. Maybe the Troop Leaders aren't encouraging the girls enough. Maybe the Girl Scout organization isn't promoting the Gold enough or in the right manner. Quite possibly it's a combination of all that and more.

Whatever the case, perhaps this book can help a few more girls achieve the Bronze, Silver and Gold! These prestigious awards **are** a time investment, but certainly not a monumental undertaking. With a bit of organization and planning, they can be a fun and so very worthwhile endeavor.

According to the "Go Gold" Brochure, 82% of girls that earn the Bronze, and 96% of girls that earn Silver, will go on to earn the Gold. (1) So earning the Bronze or Silver is a stepping stone through the gateway to Gold.

The Bronze and Silver help prepare girls for Gold by first working as a troop, then as a small group, before working individually. The suggested time requirements gradually increase. Certain components are only *considered* in the lower levels, before becoming requirements at the Gold level. Girls basically follow the same blueprint for all three awards. So by earning the Bronze and/or the Silver, attaining the Gold becomes much easier.

The deadline for earning each of these Awards is Sept 30. So for the Bronze, girls must complete their Project and turn in their Report Form by Sept

30 of the year that they complete 5th grade. For Silver, it's the year that the girl completes 8th grade and for Gold, it's the Sept 30 after graduating. In other words, girls have the entire summer after they complete the respective grade level.

However, each Council has their own deadline for inclusion in that year's annual Award Ceremony. If a girl misses the deadline for that year's Ceremony, she will be recognized in the following year's Ceremony.

These Awards are done to the best of the girl's ability, so there are no special requirements for girls with disabilities. ANY girl can earn these Awards!

Although these awards have national standards for completion, many Councils have differences when it comes to classes/workshops, reports, rules for finances, etc.

Because verifying requirements for over 100 Councils would be a monumental task resulting in a tome far greater than the size of this book, and because Council requirements often change, use this book as a guideline only and be sure to check with your Council for any Council-specific requirements.

The Bronze Award

The Bronze Award is the third highest award that can be earned in Girl Scouts. GSUSA introduced this award in 2001 for girls at the Junior level. It is a leadership award that requires a "Take Action" Project. Earning the Bronze Award helps prepare girls to earn the higher awards.

This award is earned as a troop or as part of a team, but **each** girl should put a minimum of 20 hours into the project. However, in most Councils, this is only a "suggested" minimum. It is not a hard and fast rule. Each girl needs to keep track of her hours from the beginning. Hours are counted for assembling a team, planning the Project, putting the plan into motion, educating others about the Project and inspiring others with the results. So 20 hours is not a difficult number to reach. Each Project is unique so the nature and scope of the Project, the size of the team, and the level of community involvement will all be taken into consideration. The emphasis should be on completing a quality Project, not checking off a certain number of hours.

Girls must first complete one of the Junior Journeys, to include all the awards and the required Take Action Project, that is the culmination of every Journey. Currently, the Junior Journeys include: Agent of Change, Get Moving, aMUSE, Think Like an Engineer, Think Like a Programmer, Think Like a Citizen Scientist and the Outdoor Journey.

Many Councils offer a "Journey in a Day", where girls can complete the Journey requirement in that one session. Otherwise, a Journey can easily take a troop an entire scout year to finish. Since the Junior level is only two years, the best plan of action is for the troop to complete a Journey in the first year and work on their Bronze Project the second year.

If a scout has a Troop Leader that is not doing a Journey with the troop, parents may complete the Journey at home with their child. Many of the

Journey books are sold in the Council shops for $7. The entire book does not need to be completed, although girls might find the activities in the "workbook" interesting. Each of the Journey books has a chart or planner near the back that outlines all the steps to earning the Journey Awards, to include which specific activities in the book are required. Many of the Leader Guides are packaged together with a copy of the Journey book and sold in the Council shops for about $11. The Leader Guide is not required but it will assist a parent in understanding the purpose of the Journey, as well as how to facilitate it.

Not all Troop Leaders plan to complete the Bronze Award with their troops! If a scout's Leader isn't doing the Bronze Award as a troop, try to find other Juniors who are interested in doing a Project. There may be a couple of girls in the troop that are interested. If not, ask the Leader to put you in contact with other Leaders that have Junior girls, or your Service Unit Manager, who may assist in finding girls to work with. If a troop is not completing the Bronze, the parent needs to be proactive in finding other Juniors. Call your local Council Office if you must! Do not let it deter you from earning the Bronze! If no interested Juniors can be located, a girl can team with other non-Girl Scout girls her age who may want to join GS.

Team-building is a part of earning the Bronze Award. Girls should spend some time doing team activities to encourage cooperative learning and to learn how to conquer challenges and resolve conflicts as a group.

Most Councils do not offer informational Bronze Award Workshops or Classes. If yours does, it should be beneficial to attend.

Some Councils have a "Proposal" Form that needs to be completed prior to starting a Bronze Award. Many Councils do not. These forms ask for basic personal information, a list of team members, the title of the project, the issue that will be addressed, and a brief project description.

For their Project, girls should consider their strengths and interests; and explore their community for areas where they can make a difference. What problems can be fixed? What can be improved? What would make life better/easier? What needs to be taught? What awareness needs to be raised?

At the Bronze level, Projects **can** be of benefit to the Girl Scout organization. In other words, girls can do a Project for Girl Scouts…such as planning, organizing and hosting a Girl Scout event or creating a new Girl Scout Patch Program.

Girls must understand the difference between a community service project and a Take Action Project. A community service project is usually a one-time opportunity that addresses an immediate need. It stops when the girl stops. For example, any collection drive is considered a community service project. The donations are collected and delivered. The project is over.

By contrast, a Take Action Project identifies the root cause of a problem and addresses it with a long-term solution that has measurable benefits. For example, a beach cleanup is a community service project. It helps, but it doesn't solve the problem. Installing trash cans along a stretch of beach would be a Take Action Project that may not completely end the problem, but would be a long-term solution that would result in a measureable decrease in the amount of garbage on the beach.

Ideas for Bronze Award Projects can be found in a later section of this book.

Once girls identify their top Project idea, they should discuss where to get more information, such as newspapers, magazines, online, at community events, or from people who are involved in the types of organizations that would benefit from the project.

It may be surprising how difficult it can be to find an organization that is willing to work with you! Be sure to identify who your Project will help. If it's an organization, be certain that they "want" the assistance you're planning to provide. Some places will have certain rules that might prohibit girls from completing a Project, for instance, age restrictions. Many times, an organization will suggest project ideas that they need and would welcome.

Girls should be clear on the following: the goal for the Project, the necessary steps to completion, who can assist, how others can get involved, what supplies are needed, what donations are needed and how will they be obtained.

Bronze Award Checklist

Generally, it's the Troop Leader who "approves" the Bronze Award Project. A short checklist might include:

O Do girls care about and are they excited about the Project?

O Does the Project address a need in the community?

O Can girls explain what they want to do and why it matters? Who will benefit?

O Do girls have a plan for obtaining any needed materials?

O Have the girls completed a budget and considered how they will fund it?

O When complete, how will girls know they made a difference?

At this level, Projects are not **required** to have longevity, but girls should consider how their Project *might* be sustainable and continue into the future after the current girls have finished. How can others continue the Project? For example, a Project that creates a one-day educational event at a local library, could have longevity or sustainability if it continued to be held every year by the library staff. Again, at the Bronze level, girls wouldn't be required to get confirmation from the library that they would continue the program. But the longevity component IS required for the Gold, so girls should at least have an idea of how to make a project sustainable. Council Final Report forms may also ask girls how their Project could be made sustainable.

A Project that focuses on education or raising awareness almost always fulfills the longevity component, as does a Project that leaves behind a tangible object, such as a mural or a bench.

When you educate someone or raise their awareness, they retain that knowledge for life. They may act on that knowledge. They may educate and/or inspire others to act. So the Project's affects continue to ripple on through the community, long after the Project has been completed.

Upon completion of the Project, girls should also motivate and inspire others by telling the story of what they accomplished. This can be done by visiting younger troops, making a posterboard to display at a Leader Meeting or at Council, posting on your Council's or WAGGGS webpages, sending an article to a local newspaper, etc.

Most Councils require **each** girl to submit a Final Report in order to receive the Award. These reports usually include basic personal information, the name of the Project, the problem it addressed, what the Project entailed, why girls chose the Project, what leadership skills were used, what they learned, a list of any materials/expenses, as well as a time log of hours spent on the Project. Some reports also ask how girls educated/inspired others and how the Project could be made sustainable.

Many Councils also require documentation and photographs of the Project. If this is a requirement in your Council, it usually takes the form of a scrapbook. ONE scrapbook can be submitted for all the girls.

Some Councils host an Awards Ceremony where the Bronze Awards are bestowed on the girls. In other Councils, the Service Units or Troop Leaders purchase and present the Awards. The Bronze Pin costs $8, but can't be purchased without Council certification.

The Silver Award

The Silver Award is the second highest award that can be earned in Girl Scouts. GSUSA introduced this award in 1980. It is a leadership award at the Cadette level that requires a "Take Action" Project.

This award can either be earned in a small group of 3-4 girls or as an individual. Each girl needs to track only **her** hours and **each** should put a minimum of 50 hours into the project. However, as with the Bronze, in most Councils this is only a "suggested" minimum. It is not a hard and fast rule. Each Project is unique so the nature and scope of the Project, the size of the team, and the level of community involvement will all be taken into consideration. The emphasis should be on completing a quality Project, not checking off a certain number of hours.

Girls must first complete one of the Cadette Journeys, to include all the awards and the required

Take Action Project that is the culmination of every Journey. Currently, the Cadette Journeys include: MEdia, Breathe, aMAZE, Think Like an Engineer, Think Like a Programmer, and the Outdoor Journey.

Many Councils offer a "Journey in a Day", where girls can complete the Journey requirement in that one session. Otherwise, a Journey can easily take a troop an entire scout year to finish.

If a scout has a Troop Leader that is not doing a Journey with the troop, parents may complete the Journey at home with their child. Many of the Journey books are sold in the Council shops for $7. The entire book does not need to be completed, although girls might find the activities in the "workbook" interesting. Each of the Journey books has a chart or planner near the back that outlines all the steps to earning the Journey Awards, to include which specific activities in the book are required. Many of the Leader Guides are packaged together with a copy of the Journey book and sold in the

Council shops for about $11. The Leader Guide is not required but it will assist a parent in understanding the purpose of the Journey, as well as how to facilitate it.

Girls do not need to earn the Bronze Award in order to earn the Silver.

Some Councils provide an optional informational class on the Silver Award for girls who are interested in earning it. If a scout is able to attend one of these workshops, it should be of benefit.

Councils require girls to complete a Silver Award Proposal Form, which needs to be approved, prior to starting a Silver Project.

For the Silver Award, girls should consider their interests and explore their community for areas where they can make a difference with their Project. What problems can be fixed? What can be improved? What would make your life better/easier? What needs to be taught? What awareness needs to be raised?

At the Silver level, Projects should NOT be of benefit to Girl Scouts. Projects should benefit the community.

It may be surprising how difficult it can be to find an organization that is willing to work with you! Be sure to identify who your Project will help. If it's an organization, be certain that they "want" the assistance you're planning to provide. Some places will have certain rules that might prohibit girls from completing a Project, such as age restrictions. Many times, an organization will suggest project ideas that they need and would welcome.

Ideas for Silver Award Projects can be found in a later section of this book.

Girls should be clear on the following: the goal for the Project, who can assist, how others can get involved, what supplies are needed, what donations are needed and how will they be obtained, etc.

Girls must understand the difference between a community service project and a Take Action Project. A community service project is usually a one-time opportunity. It stops when the girl stops. For example, any collection drive is considered a community service project. The donations are collected and delivered. The project is over.

By contrast, a Take Action Project identifies the root cause of a problem and addresses it with a long-term solution that has measurable benefits. For example, a beach cleanup is a community service project. It helps, but it doesn't solve the problem. Installing trash cans along a stretch of beach would be a Take Action Project that may not completely end the problem, but would be a long-term solution that would result in a measureable decrease in the amount of garbage on the beach.

Silver Award Checklist

O The project is challenging & does not repeat an existing or past project.

O The project will take at least 50 hours (per girl) to complete.

O The project includes 4 or less girls. (Some Councils allow up to 5.) Each girl's role is clear.

O The project serves a community besides GS and addresses a need in that community.

O The project has a target audience and an expected impact on that target audience.

O The project shows leadership.

O The project is measurable. The impact of the project can be shown with numbers.

O The project has a plan for sustainability.

O The budget is realistic and attainable.

O The project is not a collection. If a collection drive is included, it is a minor component.

O The project does not involve raising money for another organization.

O The project includes a plan for educating and
   inspiring others to act.

At this level, Projects should plan for longevity or
sustainability. The Project should continue into the
future after the current girl(s) have finished, but it is
not required to do so. However, at the Gold level
this is an absolute requirement, so it's best if the
Silver Project shows sustainability. For example, a
Project that creates a one-day educational event at a
local library, can continue to be held every year by
the library staff.

A Project that focuses on education or raising
awareness almost always fulfills the longevity
component, as does a Project that leaves behind a
tangible object, such as a mural or a bench.

When you educate someone or raise their awareness,
they retain that knowledge for life. They may act on
that knowledge. They may educate and/or inspire
others to act. So the Project's affects continue to

ripple on through the community, long after the Project has been completed.

Upon completion of the Project, girls should also motivate and inspire others by telling the story of what they accomplished. This can be done by visiting younger troops, making a posterboard to display at a Leader Meeting or at Council, posting on your Council's or WAGGGS webpages, posting a YouTube video, sending an article to a local newspaper, creating a blog, etc.

Councils require **each** girl to complete a Silver Award Final Report in order to receive the Award. These reports usually include basic personal information, the name of the Project, the problem it addressed, what the Project entailed, why the Project was chosen, what leadership skills were used, what was learned, a list of any materials/expenses, as well as a time log of hours spent on the Project. Some reports also ask how girls educated/inspired others and how they planned for the Project to be sustainable.

Documentation and photographs of every step of the Project is required. If the Silver Project was done as a small group, only one set of documentation/photos needs to be turned in for the group.

Some Councils host an Awards Ceremony where the Silver Awards are bestowed on the girls. In other Councils, the Service Units or Troop Leaders purchase and present the Awards. There are two types of Silver Award Pins. The silver plated pin costs $8. The sterling silver pin costs $55. Neither can be purchased without Council certification.

The Gold Award

The highest award in Girl Scouts has changed names several times since its inception in 1916. It has been called the Golden Eagle of Merit, the Golden Eaglet, the Curved Bar, First Class and the Gold Award. In 1990, national delegates approved a proposal to keep the name Gold Award in perpetuity.

The Gold Award is earned by less than 6% of eligible Girl Scouts, yet over one million girls have earned the award or its equivalent since 1916.

Many equate the Girl Scout Gold Award to the Eagle Scout rank in Boy Scouts. In some ways, that's true. Both awards are the highest in their respective organizations. Both require a leadership project. Both will allow a new recruit to advance one rank in the military.

However, attaining Eagle Scout seems a far more time-consuming endeavor, based more on mastering physical and survival skills…with requirements of earning at least 21 merit badges, including camping, first aid, emergency prep, fitness, and swimming/hiking/cycling. These merit badges are quite rigorous, requiring 20 nights of camping, a 20-mile hike or a 25-mile off-road bike ride. Boys must also earn all six ranks below Eagle Scout (which can take 4-5 years) and serve in a leadership position for six months.

But many Eagle Projects seem to be more on the level of a Girl Scout Bronze or Silver Project, in that they mainly entail building/constructing or collection drives: park benches, bat houses, playgrounds, gardens, memorials, ramps, blood drives, book drives, etc.

Meanwhile, there are no badge requirements for the Gold Award, nor do girls have to earn any lower "ranks". A girl can earn the Gold without spending a single night at camp or earning a single badge, although the newer Outdoor, Programmer and

Engineer Journeys do have badges associated with them.

But some Girl Scout Gold Award Projects are absolutely astounding. In 2015, one girl taught self-defense to females in a village in India, as well as at battered women's shelters in LA, starting a non-profit called "For a Change, Defend". Another girl produced a documentary on human sex trafficking that is now used by the FBI for training purposes. A third girl started iDREAM Express, a non-profit that brings a weekly mobile learning center to the Philippines where children are bathed, educated and fed. (2)

Of course, these are the exceptional Projects. So don't let them discourage you. A Project does not need to reach around the world. The vast majority of Gold Award Projects are much simpler in scope and can be accomplished in one's own neighborhood.

The Gold Award is earned by high school girls at the Senior or Ambassador level.

This award **must** be earned as an individual. Girls should put a minimum of 80 hours into the project. However, in most Councils this is only a "suggested" minimum. It is not a hard and fast rule. Each Project is unique so the scope and nature of the Project, the size of the team, and the level of community involvement will all be taken into consideration. The emphasis should be on completing a quality Project, not ticking off a certain number of hours.

Be sure to verify what hours are allowed in your Council. Some do not allow hours spent on the Final Report or scrapbook. Travel time also can not be counted.

Girls do NOT have to do the entire Project themselves. It is a leadership Project so girls are expected to assemble volunteers to assist in carrying out certain aspects of the Project, and delegate tasks to them. **If you can do the Project alone, it's not leadership.** However, girls can not count hours that her assistants put in.

Girls must first complete two Journeys, to include all the awards and the required Take Action Projects that are the culmination of every Journey. The two Journeys can be Senior Journeys, Ambassador Journeys or one of each.

Currently, the Senior Journeys include: Girltopia, Sow What, Mission Sisterhood, Think Like an Engineer, Think Like a Programmer, and the Outdoor Journey. The Ambassador Journeys include: Your Voice Your World, Justice, Bliss, Think Like an Engineer, Think Like a Programmer and the Outdoor Journey.

Girls do not need to earn the Silver Award in order to earn the Gold. However, if a girl does earn the Silver Award, she only needs to complete ONE Senior/Ambassador Journey.

Girl are required to attend a Gold Award Workshop and complete a Gold Award Proposal Form, which must be approved, prior to beginning their Project. In most Councils, girls may not start counting their hours until AFTER their Proposal is approved. (In at least one Council, girls are allowed to count 10 hours prior to Proposal approval.)

A very informative, 17-minute Gold Award Webinar by Girl Scouts of Gulfcoast Florida can be found here:

https://www.youtube.com/watch?v=DkE7_Oansr Q&feature=youtu.be

Ideas for Gold Award Projects can be found in a later section of this book.

When choosing a Project, girls should consider their interests and explore their community for areas where they can make a difference. What problems can be fixed? What can be improved? What would make your life better/easier? What needs to be taught?

It may be surprising how difficult it can be to find an organization that is willing to work with you! Be sure to identify who your Project will help. If it's an organization, be certain that they "want" the assistance you're planning to provide. Many times, an organization will suggest project ideas that they need and would welcome.

At the Gold level, Projects can NOT be of benefit to Girl Scouts. Projects should benefit the community.

Girls must understand the difference between a community service project and a Take Action Project. A community service project is usually a one-time opportunity. It stops when the girl stops. For example, any collection drive is considered a community service project. The donations are collected and delivered. The project is over.

By contrast, a Take Action Project identifies the root cause of a problem and addresses it with a long-term solution that has measurable benefits. For example, a beach cleanup is a community service project. It helps, but it doesn't solve the problem. Installing trash cans along a stretch of beach would be a Take Action Project that may not completely end the problem, but would be a long-term solution that would result in a measureable decrease in the amount of garbage on the beach.

The best strategy is to not stress over the Proposal. Girls often get derailed because they fret too much at the Proposal stage and they never submit it. The Proposal is a *plan*. Just get it filled out and submitted. Councils almost never say "no". If a Project isn't robust enough, if it doesn't have sustainability, if it's too broad or too small…whatever the deficiency, Council does not want to ever say "no". They will either say "yes" or they will respond with a request for revision. They will specify what needs to be done to bring the proposed Project "up to snuff". In that case, take the Proposal back to the drawing board and flesh out the component that is lacking and resubmit! Do this as often as it takes to get the green light!

Be sure to complete the Gold Award Checklist in this book and your Proposal should pass with flying colors!

Some Councils require girls to attend an interview with an approval committee before their Project can be approved!

Girls can submit their Proposal Form online at the GoGold website:
https://www.girlscouts.org/gogoldonline/

Some Councils also still allow paper Proposal Forms. These Forms may differ, but should be based on GSUSAs Form, found here:

https://www.girlscouts.org/content/dam/girlscouts-gsusa/forms-and-documents/our-

program/Gold%20Award/Girl_Scout_Gold_Award
_Proposal.pdf

On the Proposal Form, a Project Advisor will need to be selected. This is the "expert" in the field relating to the Project. For instance, a Culinary Project might have a Chef as the Project Advisor. An Education Project might have a teacher, principal or librarian as the Project Advisor. It could be someone who works at the organization that is benefitting from the Project. The Project Advisor is rarely a member of Girl Scouts and is never related to you.

The form will also ask for people/organizations you plan to work with, the issue, the target audience, why the project was chosen, talents/skills to be used and those to be learned, plan of action, materials needed, approvals needed, expenses, how the impact will be evaluated, how the project will be sustained, and how others will be inspired.

At this level, Projects **must** have longevity or sustainability. The Project must continue into the future after the current girl has finished. For example, a Project that creates a one-day educational event at a local library, must continue to be held every year by the library staff or other entity.

A Project that focuses on education or raising awareness almost always becomes sustainable, as does a Project that leaves behind a tangible object, such as a mural or a bench.

When you educate someone or raise their awareness, they retain that knowledge for life. They may act on that knowledge. They may educate and/or inspire others to act. So the Project's affects continue to ripple on through the community, long after the Project has been completed.

Projects should also have an educational aspect to them and girls should motivate and inspire others by telling the story of what they accomplished. This can be done by visiting younger troops, speaking at a

Leader Meeting or at Council, posting on your Council's or WAGGGS webpages, sending an article to a local newspaper, creating a blog, posting a video on YouTube, etc.

Gold Award Checklist

O My project challenges me & does not repeat an existing or past project.

O My project will take at least 80 hours to complete.

O My Project Advisor has specific knowledge of my topic and is NOT related to me.

O My project serves a community besides GS.

O My project addresses a need in the community.

O My project has a target audience and an expected impact on that target audience.

O My project shows leadership – networking, scheduling, organizing a team, leading others.

O My project is measurable. I will be able to show the impact of my project with numbers.

O My project is sustainable and will continue to have an impact once I am no longer involved.

O My budget is realistic and attainable.

O My project is not a collection. If a collection drive is included, it is a minor component.

O My project does not involve raising money for another organization.

O My project's issue has a national or global link.

O My project includes a plan for educating and
    inspiring others to act.

For the national/global link, girls should either:

1) Find a similar project in another
    community/country and reach out to them
    for ideas or advice on how to successfully
    implement their Gold Project.

2) Give someone else the ability to recreate and
    implement the Gold Project in their
    community. This can be accomplished
    through flyers, brochures, videos,
    presentations, social media, etc. It should
    include any of the following: step-by-step
    instructions, advice, lessons learned, positive
    feedback from participants, etc.

Once the Proposal Form is approved, Council will assign a Gold Award Advisor, or sometimes called a Gold Award Mentor. This is different from the Project Advisor. This is a Council volunteer who is versed in the Gold Award requirements and procedures.

It is the *girl's* responsibility to contact the Advisor and communicate with them throughout the Project. In many Councils, the Advisor isn't even allowed to have any communication with the parent!

The Advisor is there to assist with any issues, problems or questions. They can provide support, encouragement and oftentimes, motivation. However, the relationship is driven by the *girl*. If a girl does not reach out to her Advisor, they may have very little involvement. In some Councils there is a specific requirement for how often a girl must communicate with her Advisor.

Communication with the Advisor does not have to be face-to-face meetings. With the busy schedules of today's high schoolers, it is most often done via email or text messages. But it is the Advisor that signs off on the Project...ultimately approves it...so it's in one's best interest to keep them in the loop.

My older daughter emailed her Advisor a couple times, but never met her until the Project was complete and needed the Advisor's signature.

My youngest daughter had an approved Gold Award Project last year, but it ended up being one she wasn't really interested in. (See chapter on Helicopter Parents...lol.) I don't even know if she ever communicated with her Advisor! But she ended up scrapping that Project and is now pulling together another one in line with her passion.

The first girl I was assigned to as an Advisor checked in via email periodically to update me on her status and ask questions. I wanted to attend her Project workshop on 3D printers, but she never notified me of the date. So we never met until the Gold Award Ceremony! We ended up doing everything via email.

Another girl I was assigned to kept in touch via text messages. We had very little interaction. At the end of her Project, we did meet to go over her scrapbook and time log, so I could sign off on her Project.

Girls must complete a Final Report in order to receive the Award. This can be done on the GoGold website, or some Councils still accept paper forms. The submission must include documentation and photos of every step of the Project, along with a time log of hours spent on the Project. In some Councils the documentation/photos can take the form of a physical scrapbook or digital files.

Some Councils have their own Final Report, but it should be based on GSUSA's form. Some of the questions can be difficult. It's best to get familiar with the Final Report at the start of the Project. The form will ask: what was done and why, what was the impact, who benefitted, what was the root cause of the issue addressed, how is it sustainable, what obstacles were encountered, how were they overcome, how were others inspired, and what was learned. It may ask about national or global links…ways in which your project might have global implications because it addresses an issue that is found worldwide.

The GSUSA Final Report can be found here:

https://www.girlscouts.org/content/dam/girlscouts-gsusa/forms-and-documents/our-program/Gold%20Award/Girl_Scout_Gold_Award_Final_Report.pdf

The Advisor must sign the Final Report. In most Councils, *once signed by the Advisor, the Project is considered approved and the girl is considered a Gold Award Recipient.*

Most Councils hold an annual Gold Award Ceremony where girls receive the actual award.

There are two types of pins. The gold tone pin is $18.50 and the gold filled pin is $50. There is also a mini "Parent Gold Award Pin" for $20.50. These can not be purchased from the Girl Scout Shop without Council approval.

Councils provide the Gold Award Pin to their recipients. So you should not need to purchase one.

National Young Women of Distinction

Every year, Girl Scouts honors ten extraordinary girls as National Young Women of Distinction. They are chosen because their Gold Award Projects demonstrate extraordinary leadership, have measurable impact and sustainability, igniting change in their communities and/or around the world.

"Our National Young Women of Distinction have demonstrated remarkable leadership through their extraordinary Take Action projects," said Anna Maria Chávez, CEO of Girl Scouts of the USA. "At such a young age, these girls are creating positive change in their communities, identifying local solutions that relate to global issues, and taking sustainable action to make a difference in the world. We are proud to recognize the contributions and achievements of these exceptional girls and cannot wait to see how they continue to inspire, influence, and innovate as the leaders and social entrepreneurs of tomorrow." (2)

In order to be considered for the National Young Women of Distinction, a girl must submit her Gold Award Project through the GoGold website!

Honorees receive professional public speaking training and represent GSUSA as speakers at a number of local and national events. They are awarded $15,000 scholarships and other opportunities to sustain their Gold Award Projects.

In addition to the three 2015 Projects listed here, in the section on the Gold Award, some of the 2017 NYWOD recipients were:

One girl developed a soil moisture sensor to help rural farmers conserve 25% more water. She received a provisional patent on her product.

One girl provided a sanitary pad machine to a rural village in India, which grinds cotton, presses it into pads and disinfects them. She conducted workshops in the surrounding villages on menstrual hygiene.

Another girl established a non-profit organization and successfully lobbied to get New York State legislators to pass legislation to protect bee populations.

Another girl secured donations of hand sanitizer, created posters and brochures, and conducted four lectures in China. Her efforts led the local government to provide hand sanitizer to the community's hospitals. (3)

Monetary Rules

If a Bronze/Silver/Gold Award Project requires funding, a money-earning project may be used. All money-earning projects need to be approved by Council, by submitting a Money-Earning Application at least four weeks prior to the event. (Some Councils require even more time.)

Councils require girls to participate in Council Product Sales, before any additional money-earning projects will be approved. Girls can use profits from their Council Product Sales.

Girls may not raise money for other organizations, but they may donate a portion of their troop funds to worthwhile projects or organizations. Girls may not sell commercial products such as candy bars, cookie dough, pizzas, etc. Girls may not hold product demonstration "parties" like Tupperware or Pampered Chef. Girls may not hold raffles/drawings or other games of chance.

The allowance of restaurant nights varies by Council.

The rules for donations can be tedious and seem to vary from Council to Council.

Girls may not directly solicit cash donations, but in most Councils adults are allowed to "do the asking". Generally, if a cash donation exceeds a certain amount, usually $250, it must be sent to Council and then distributed through the girl's troop.

The rules for in-kind donations seem to vary by Council. A few seem to allow girls to ask for material or service donations, most only allow adults to do so. Again, if the donation exceeds $250 in value, it needs to be reported to Council.

Girls may describe their Project, write letters, create Powerpoint presentations, but an adult must do the actual asking and the adult should sign all letters/emails. It must be made clear to the donor that it is for a Gold Award Project and is not tax-deductible.

Grants need to be approved and coordinated with Council.

Some examples of allowable money-earning projects are: car washes, garage sales, holiday gift wrapping, bake sales, spaghetti dinners, face painting, hosting GS events like a dance or badge workshop.

These projects can not take place during the Council's Product Sales.

Choosing a Project

One way to choose a project is to approach a local organization and ask them if there's a need that you can turn into a project. Many organizations have projects they'd love to have done. They just don't have the volunteers or the means of making it happen.

My older daughter had been volunteering for six months at Bit-by-Bit Therapeutic Riding Center, when she approached one of the therapists and asked if there was a project she could do. They were thrilled, and suggested she make dressage boards and build a sensory trail. Although there was a setback, which is mentioned in the "When Plans Go Awry" section, this became her Gold Award Project.

On the other hand, my younger daughter's first idea for a Silver Project was to do something for Canine Companions, an organization that trained service dogs. But, unfortunately, the organization was based in Orlando, over 200 miles away, and getting anyone interested in working with her proved impossible.

Another way to choose a project is to come up with a project idea first and then find an organization to work with. This can often be a more difficult prospect, since it involves finding an organization that not only is willing to work with you but also wants what you are offering.

My youngest daughter's second idea for a Silver Project involved doing crafts with sick kids. But she had problems getting two different hospitals to work with her. So she had to reach out to my network of Troop Leaders and ask if any of them knew of an organization that would be interested in her Project. Thankfully, two of them responded and she was able to do her Project at both locations.

Because these projects require dedication and perseverance, girls are most successful when they choose a project that they are interested in and passionate about. It shouldn't be what the Troop

Leader is interested in. It shouldn't be what the parents are interested in. But what the girl(s) are passionate about.

Pick a passion: art, music, sports, fashion, cooking, animal welfare, photography, nature, finance, science, design, coding, travel...

Some girls have a friend or relative with an illness or disease, so they choose to do a project involving that.

The best projects usually have more than one component to them. For example, a Gold Award Literacy Project might involve speaking to local organizations about literacy, collecting books, building book shelves and making pillows for a book nook, creating a tutoring program with volunteer recruits and providing a weekly storytime. This project has a little bit of everything, and it fulfills all the requirements. It raises awareness and educates. It meets the longevity/sustainability in three ways: the books, shelves and pillows will continue to be used for years to come; the tutoring program will continue to be run by volunteers; and by speaking to organizations, individual awareness is raised which inspires others to act.

Project Ideas

To view an interactive map of Girl Scout Bronze, Silver and Gold Awards, visit: https://www.girlscouts.org/en/for-girls/girls-changing-the-world.html

Included here are various projects from Girls Scouts of Southeast Florida (GSSEF):

<u>Bronze Award Projects:</u>

"Meals on Wheels" - One troop made placemats and decorations on several holidays for Meals on Wheels recipients. They also collected and bagged petfood, collected plastic grocery bags, and held a food drive. They raised awareness throughout their Service Unit and inspired other troops to also complete projects for Meals on Wheels.

"Bat Boxes" – This troop made and installed box houses for bats at a local park.

"Lobby Design" – This troop designed the waiting area in the lobby of a local foster care office. They also provided children's books and duffel bags filled with the basic necessities needed when children are removed from their homes on short notice.

"Graceful Garden" – This troop designed and planted a garden at the church where they hold their troop meetings.

Silver Award Projects:

"Reading is Essential" – This troop provided a weekly summer storytime at their local library and at a local preschool. They collected hundreds of books which were donated to both the preschool and a children's hospital. They also made pillows for the reading nook at the preschool.

"Krafty Kids" – This girl took her Project to two organizations. Every week during the summer, she visited a Hispanic preschool at an organization for immigrants and refugees, and donated a children's picture book which was read to the students in English. Afterwards, she led a craft related to the storybook. She also paid weekly visits to a foster children's village and did crafts with the children. She donated a cart full of craft supplies for the children to use during the week.

Gold Award Projects:

"Music is Elementary" – This girl loved music so for her Project she wanted to provide an exciting and engaging way for students to learn about music. She teamed with fellow band students to create a DVD series for music teachers that showed a variety of instruments, information about playing them and demonstrations of how each is played.

"All Stressed Out" – This girl addressed teen stress by developing a workshop to help teens identify what was causing them anxiety and stress. The workshop also offered local resources. A presentation was also put on YouTube so teens everywhere could access it.

"Sewing for Smiles" – This girl put her passion for sewing into her Project. She led workshops to teach people of all ages to sew. The students in her workshops then handmade nearly 300 pillowcases for a local children's hospital.

"Importance of Coral Reefs" – This scout used her passion for environmental science to create an elementary school education program about coral reefs. The program included egg carton coral reefs, jello-mold habitats, lessons with bubbles and EnviroScapes made with cocoa powder, food coloring and sprinkles. She held three community events using her curriculum. Her community partners continued to utilize her activities in future programs.

"Imagination Playground" – This scout installed a playground at a local children's museum.

"Tutus and Tool Belts" – addressing the established gender roles that can create barriers for girls to explore traditional male-dominated subjects, this scout created seven classes focused on chemistry, physics, gravity, electricity and robotics which she presented to eager girls at a local school.

"Raising Service Dogs" – this scout became a volunteer in a Puppy Raising Program. The 18-month commitment involved obedience training, grooming requirements, vet appointments and home inspections. She also brought awareness to her school, friends, community and scouts about the benefits of training animals to serve.

"Prescription Addiction" – this girl developed a presentation for the elderly, along with a DVD and an information packet to educate them on the dangers of prescription medication overuse and misuse. Her materials were used several times with local organizations in her community.

"Free Library" – this Project addressed the need for quality books and reading materials. The scout built two lending library structures for children and filled them with over 300 donated books.

"Littles Remodeled" – this scout created bright, kid-friendly designs to decorate a play area at a local organization for children who suffered the death of a loved one.

"BRACE Yourself for College" – this scout developed a website, a school bulletin board and an education booth at Freshmen orientation to ensure that students were aware of free tools, services and resources available for secondary education.

"Sense-Ability Trail" – this scout volunteered for a year at an equestrian therapeutic riding center before creating part of a trail to stimulate the sight and smell of the riders. She created dressage boards with not only the traditional letters, but also colors and animal pictures. She also created a scent station where riders can stop and smell four different essential oils.

"Liquidate Lionfish" – this scout created a program to educate the public on the invasive lionfish. She spent several weekends at a booth at a national park where she spoke to hundreds of visitors. She also created an educational truck which included posters, a 3D model, brochures and stickers for the rangers to use as teaching tools for outreach programs.

Helicopter Parents

As a homeschooling parent and a Troop Leader, I've had the most difficult time in resisting the urge of the "helicopter parent", in that I often find myself…egads…doing tasks that my girls can and should be doing themselves! Now, to be fair, I do have a child with Social Anxiety, who can not speak on the phone if her life depended upon it. So, yes, I have to confess, I did have to make some of those calls for her while she was working on her Gold Award. But there have been other times when I've spun my rotors too.

At a Gold Award Advisor training, the Council representative said that you can often spot the "helicopter parents" when they refer to their child's project using the term "we", instead of "she":

"We contacted the organization."

"We shopped for the supplies."

"We had a problem with…"

It shouldn't be "we", but "she".

Parents CAN be cheerleaders. Parents CAN be coaches. Parents CAN be chauffeurs. But parents can NOT be taskmasters.

So parents, and Leaders, if you're reading this…don't hover around. "We" are not an integral part of "our" project.

It is definitely a fine line, because girls do need encouragement, support, and very often a little kick in the…or shall I say…nudge in the right direction. They get distracted. They get lazy. They get discouraged. They get swamped with all the other activities in their lives.

But rather than being a "helicopter parent", be instead a fighter pilot. Come screaming over the horizon, afterburners glowing, and buzz the tower to get their attention, before heading off into the sunset.

When Plans Go Awry

Girls need to be flexible when their Project goes awry. It happens all too often and girls should expect it! Part of the learning process of these Awards is to overcome obstacles. Just because a Project doesn't have the anticipated outcome, doesn't mean the award can't still be earned. By documenting all problems, issues and obstacles, along with how they were addressed and/or overcome, girls can still be awarded for their perseverance and tenacity.

For example, one girl's Project addressed homelessness and hunger. She formed a team of volunteers to cook, package and serve meals to the homeless on the weekend. Part-way through her project, the city enacted a law prohibiting the serving of *cooked* food to the homeless in public places. Rather than giving up, she changed the direction of her project and began making and serving sandwiches.

My older daughter's Gold Award Project ended up being only a portion of what was planned. She approached the organization for ideas in Dec, BEFORE she had finished her Journey. They wanted her to make a sensory trail with four stations to stimulate sight, sound, smell and touch. She had her Project Proposal all ready to submit. But it was another FIVE MONTHS before her troop finally finished the Journey! By then, the organization had hired someone to make the sound and touch components. Luckily, she was able to acquire the suggested 80 hours by making the other two components and the Award was still approved.

As I mentioned earlier, my younger daughter's Silver Project involved doing weekly crafts with patients at a local children's hospital. Because the Project was planned for winter, visits became impossible due to frequent quarantines of the ward. Other times she

was told there weren't enough children in the ward.
Then the woman in charge of volunteers had a leave
of absence due to a health issue! So my daughter
was no longer able to do her Project at that time.
When she decided to move the Project to the
summer months, she learned that the hospital
already had people coming to do crafts during the
summer months. So, she took her craft Project to
two alternate locations. One was a Hispanic
preschool and the other was a foster care children's
village. The preschool crafts were based on different
children's books, which she also donated to the
classroom. The home at the children's village
received a craft cart filled with supplies for the kids
to use during the week.

The most important thing to do when Projects go
awry is to contact the Gold Award Advisor. They
can help get it back on track. Any changes have to
be approved by Council.

Gold Award Scholarships

According to College Scholarships.org, "Organizations like Girl Scouts of the USA provide valuable resume entries for financial aid seekers who want to stand out. Membership in scouting organizations illustrates your commitment to excellence, and shows scholarship administrators that you are serious about education. No matter where you compete for aid, your scouting affiliation gives you a leg up."

There are numerous scholarships out there specifically for scouts that have earned the Gold Award. Many Councils list local scholarships on their website. Included here are only a few for illustration:

The American Legion offers a $1000 GS Achievement Award for Gold Awardees.

The Corinne Jeannine Schillings Foundation Scholarship distributes financial aid to Gold or Silver Awardees who plan to major in a foreign language.

The Elks Foundation provides 8 Gold Awardee scholarships each worth $6000.

Albright College (Reading, PA) offers a $500 scholarship for Gold Awardees.

Lebanon Valley College offers up to $2000 to Gold Awardees.

Trinity Washington University awards $5000 scholarships for Gold Awardees and $4000 scholarships for Silver Awardees.

Veterans of Foreign Wars awards 3 Scout of the Year scholarships to Gold Awardees in the amounts of $1000, $3000 and $5000.

Lipscomb University has a $2500 Scout Award for Gold Awardees. It is renewable up to 8 semesters.

Notes

(1) GoGold Brochure

https://www.girlscouts.org/content/dam/girlscouts-gsusa/forms-and-documents/about-girl-scouts/advocacy/GoGold_Brochure.pdf

(2) 2015 National Young Women of Distinction news release, https://www.girlscouts.org/en/press-room/press-room/news-releases/2015/2015-NYWOD.html

(3) 2017 National Young Women of Distinction news release,

https://www.girlscouts.org/en/press-room/press-room/news-releases/2017/GSUSA-announces-2017-national-young-women-of-distinction.html

It is impossible for me to address herein, all the various tidbits of information/advice that I have from my 26 years in GS. If you have questions, need further explanation or have an issue not covered in this book, please email me at: kindredsoul65@gmail.com

Printed by Amazon Italia Logistica S.r.l.
Torrazza Piemonte (TO), Italy

48324956R00045